The INSIDE GUIDE

CIVIL RIGHTS HEROES

Malcolm X

By Amy B. Rogers

Cavendish Square
New York

Published in 2022 by Cavendish Square Publishing, LLC
29 E. 21st Street, New York, NY 10010

First Edition

Portions of this work were originally authored by Barbara M. Linde and published as *Malcolm X (Civil Rights Crusaders)*. All new material this edition authored by Amy B. Rogers..

Library of Congress Cataloging-in-Publication Data

Names: Rogers, Amy B., author.
Title: Malcolm X / Amy B. Rogers.
Description: New York : Cavendish Square Publishing, [2022] | Series: The inside guide: Civil Rights heroes | Includes bibliographical references and index.
Identifiers: LCCN 2020028376 | ISBN 9781502660121 (library binding) | ISBN 9781502660107 (paperback) | ISBN 9781502660114 (set) | ISBN 9781502660138 (ebook)
Subjects: LCSH: X, Malcolm, 1925-1965–Juvenile literature. | African American civil rights workers–Biography–Juvenile literature. | African American Muslims–Biography–Juvenile literature. | Black Muslims–Biography–Juvenile literature. | Civil rights–United States–History–Juvenile literature.
Classification: LCC E185.97.L5 R64 2022 | DDC 320.54/6092 [B]–dc23
LC record available at https://lccn.loc.gov/2020028376

Editor: Katie Kawa
Copy Editor: Abby Young
Designer: Andrea Davison-Bartolotta

The photographs in this book are used by permission and through the courtesy of: Cover, pp. 6, 12, 22, 28 (bottom left, top right) Bettmann/Getty Images; p. 4 Bob Parent/Hulton Archive/Getty Images; p. 7 Underwood Archives/Getty Images; p. 8 William Lovelace/Express/Getty Images; p. 9 Lev Radin/Pacific Press/LightRocket via Getty Images; pp. 10, 28 (top left) Afro American Newspapers/Gado/Getty Images; p. 13 Hulton Archive/Getty Images; p. 14 Abdel Ghani Bashir/AFP via Getty Images; p. 15 Bob Gomel/The LIFE Images Collection via Getty Images/Getty Images; p. 16 Robert Parent/The LIFE Images Collection via Getty Images/Getty Images; p. 18 Ira L. Black/Corbis via Getty Images; pp. 19, 20 Michael Ochs Archives/Getty Images; p. 21 Pictorial Parade/Getty Images; p. 24 Tayfun Coskun/Anadolu Agency/Getty Images; p. 25 Hulton Deutsch/Corbis Historical/Getty Images; p. 26 Largo International NV/Getty Images; p. 27 Kevin Mazur/Getty Images for Coachella/Getty Images; p. 28 (bottom right) Francis Miller/The LIFE Picture Collection via Getty Images; p. 29 (top) Frank Scherschel/The LIFE Picture Collection via Getty Images; p. 29 (bottom) Thabo Jaiyesimi/SOPA Images/LightRocket via Getty Images.

CPSIA compliance information: Batch #CS22CSQ: For further information contact Cavendish Square Publishing LLC, New York, New York, at 1-877-980-4450.

Printed in the United States of America

CONTENTS

Malcolm X was one of the most influential speakers of his time, and his words still inspire people today.

A POWERFUL VOICE

Chapter One

The 1950s and 1960s were decades of change for all Americans, but especially for Black Americans. Black leaders called attention to the problem of racism in the United States, and more people started listening. Each of these leaders had their own voice and their own hopes for a better future for Black Americans. Malcolm X was one such leader with a very powerful voice.

> **Fast Fact**
>
> Racism is the belief that one race is better than others and should have power over other races. It also refers to the political and social systems that keep one race in power over others.

A Different Opinion

Malcolm X grew up surrounded by racism and violence against Black Americans. He knew the problems Black Americans were facing, and it made him angry. This anger influenced his speeches throughout his life as an activist. He often called for more forceful actions than those of other

Black leaders, such as Dr. Martin Luther King Jr., who organized peaceful protests.

While other leaders fought for **integration**, Malcolm called for Black people to stand on their own. He believed integration wasn't good for Black Americans.

Fast Fact

Martin Luther King Jr. and Malcolm X met only once. The meeting occurred on March 26, 1964, and lasted only about a minute.

Malcolm X (*right*) and Martin Luther King Jr. (*left*) were two of the most important Black leaders of the 1960s, but they were very different people with different ideas and methods.

Black Nationalism

One of the most important ideas Malcolm called attention to in his speeches was Black nationalism. This was the idea that Black people didn't need to integrate themselves into white society. Instead, they could create a separate society built on Black pride. Many Black nationalists called for the eventual creation of a separate nation for Black people. The ideas of Black pride and Black nationalism that Malcolm brought into the spotlight played a big part in the Black Power movement that grew during the 1960s and 1970s.

Malcolm called for a revolution. This made some people, especially white people, angry and uncomfortable. They wanted to keep things exactly as they were. However, many young Black Americans were inspired by his words to forcefully fight for change.

In 1963, Malcolm said, "If you're afraid of Black nationalism, you're afraid of revolution. And if you love revolution, you love Black nationalism."

A New Point of View

Malcolm's story is a story of a man with strong opinions. It's also a story of a man who wasn't afraid to change those opinions as he learned more about the world and people around him. For example, as time went on, he began to change his mind about the

Fast Fact

Around 1,500 people attended Malcolm's funeral in Harlem, which is a neighborhood in New York City that has historically been a center of Black culture.

THE CIVIL RIGHTS MOVEMENT

Malcolm's message of revolution was very different from the mostly peaceful message of the civil rights movement. This movement, which gained national attention in the 1950s and 1960s, called for an end to segregation, or the forced separation of Black people and white people in places such as schools, restaurants, and public bathrooms. The leaders of this movement, such as Martin Luther King Jr., practiced peaceful forms of protest, such as marches and **boycotts**. These nonviolent methods were criticized by Malcolm X, but the civil rights movement did achieve important victories, including an end to legal segregation.

Marches were a common form of nonviolent protest used during the civil rights movement.

civil rights movement, which focused on integration rather than Black nationalism. Instead of criticizing its leaders, such as Martin Luther King Jr., he began to think about working with them.

However, before Malcolm could really start putting these new plans into action, he was killed. On February 21, 1965, he was assassinated, or murdered, by members of a group he had once worked with.

Pride and Anger

Malcolm X's message was one of both pride and anger. He was proud to be Black and wanted other Black people to be proud of their identity too. However, he was also angry about the way Black people were being treated, and he wanted to take more forceful action to change things.

Malcolm's **legacy** lives on in the work of many Black activists today. For example, his influence was felt in protests that spread across all 50 U.S. states and many other countries in 2020. Protesters pushed for changes in the way Black people are treated, especially by police. Their pride and anger showed that Malcolm's message is still reaching people today.

Malcolm X has inspired generations of Black activists.

Malcolm's childhood was shaped by racism. He grew up with a strong understanding of the hatred and violence Black people experienced in the United States.

Chapter Two

FROM MALCOLM LITTLE TO MALCOLM X

Malcolm X's birth name was Malcolm Little. He was born on May 19, 1925, in Nebraska. The Little family faced many hard times after Malcolm was born, and those hard times influenced his future activism in important ways.

A Family Tragedy

Malcolm's father, Earl Little, was a Baptist preacher who talked about Black nationalism and Black pride. This angered many white people, including violent groups such as the Black Legion.

Malcolm's family had to move more than once to try to get away from the Black Legion. They eventually ended up in Michigan. However, they weren't safe there either. Their house was set on fire in 1929. Two years later, when Malcolm was only six years old, his father died. His family believed he had been killed by angry white people, but the police said it was an accident.

Fast Fact

Earl Little was a supporter of Marcus Garvey, who was a famous early leader of the Black nationalist movement.

Growing Up Fast

After Earl's death, Malcolm's mother, Louise, struggled with her mental and emotional health. She was eventually sent to a kind of hospital. Her seven children went to live with family members or in **foster homes**.

Although life was hard, Malcolm did well in school. He was even elected class president in junior high. However, when he was in eighth grade, he told one of his teachers he wanted to become a lawyer. The teacher told him being a carpenter was more **realistic**. Malcolm became angry. He soon dropped out of school and moved to Boston, Massachusetts.

Life in Jail

Malcolm spent time in Boston and New York City. He became involved in drug deals and **robberies**, and he was arrested in 1946 for stealing.

After Malcolm dropped out of school, he started getting in trouble. He fell deeper and deeper into a life of crime. Shown here is a mug shot, or official police photograph, taken after one of his arrests in the 1940s.

He was then sent to prison, where he renewed his love for learning and read many books.

Malcolm's brother Reginald talked to Malcolm while he was in prison. He told him about a group called the Nation of Islam (NOI) and its leader, Elijah Muhammad. As Malcolm learned more about this group, he began to follow its teachings. He stopped eating pork and smoking because it went against Islam. His entire life started to change.

Shown here is Elijah Muhammad. He became a mentor to Malcolm X after Malcolm got out of jail. A mentor is someone who teaches or gives advice to another person.

Fast Fact

While Malcolm was in jail, he wrote down every word in the dictionary and its definition, or meaning. This helped him learn many new things.

Becoming Malcolm X

The NOI was a Black nationalist organization. It taught its followers, called Black Muslims, that white people were evil and were trying to keep Black people beneath them in society. Because of this, Black Muslims

ISLAM

Malcolm X became a devout, or serious, Muslim during his time in prison. A Muslim is a person who practices the religion of Islam. The founder of Islam was Muhammad, who was born around 570 in Mecca, which is in today's Saudi Arabia. He's known as the Prophet, and Muslims believe he was given the word of God (called Allah by Muslims). The word of Allah was written down in the Muslim holy book known as the Quran. Islam is the fastest-growing religion in the world, and around 2 billion people identify as Muslims.

Every Muslim is expected to travel to Mecca once in their lifetime. This trip is known as the hajj.

believed they needed to create a state, or nation, that was separate from white people. This was the only way they thought they'd ever find true freedom and justice.

Malcolm embraced the message of the NOI. He even followed other NOI members in changing his last name. By the time he got out of prison in 1952, he was no longer Malcolm Little. He was Malcolm X.

Fast Fact

Black Muslims said their real African names were lost when past family members were enslaved, so they used X to stand for those lost names.

Malcolm X was one of many Black Muslims who changed their name after joining the NOI. For example, the real name of the famous boxer and Black Muslim Muhammad Ali was Cassius Clay. He changed his name because, like Malcolm, he believed his old name was an enslaved person's name.

Malcolm spoke his mind, and he didn't care if it made him unpopular. He said and did what he thought was right.

Chapter Three

SPEAKING HIS MIND

Malcolm was smart and a strong public speaker. His speeches inspired many people who felt the civil rights movement wasn't doing enough for Black Americans. He soon became a leader in the NOI and one of the most well-known speakers of his time.

NOI Leadership

Malcolm worked with Elijah Muhammad to bring more people to the NOI. He gave many speeches for the group, and his words made people want to join the organization. NOI membership grew from around 500 to around 30,000 during Malcolm's time with the NOI.

Malcolm served as the head of NOI temples in Boston and later in Harlem. He also served as the national representative for the group. He traveled to many parts of the United States, setting up NOI temples. He also spoke at many colleges, as well as on television and radio programs, about race.

Fast Fact

Malcolm was the founder of the NOI's newspaper, *Muhammad Speaks*. He began printing it in his basement!

"Any Means Necessary"

In Malcolm's speeches, he often talked about the need for Black people to practice self-defense. He grew up in a family that was affected by violence from white people toward Black people, and he supported the NOI's call for Black people to stand up for themselves. In fact, he said Black people should use "any means necessary" to achieve freedom and justice.

Some Black Americans were looking for an **alternative** to the more peaceful methods of the civil rights movement. To them, Malcolm X became a hero who offered a more forceful path to change.

Malcolm's belief that there can't be peace without justice is still shared by many today.

Fast Fact

In April 1964, Malcolm delivered a speech called "The Ballot or the Bullet." In this famous speech, he said that voting could be used as a kind of weapon to create change. However, he also said that if Black Americans were denied their full rights, they could rise up using actual weapons.

Losing Faith

When Malcolm discovered that Elijah Muhammad had broken some of the NOI's rules, he lost faith in his mentor. Malcolm and Elijah began to disagree about many things, and by 1964, Malcolm was officially no longer part of the NOI.

That same year, Malcolm formed his own organization—Muslim Mosque, Inc. He also spent part of that year traveling to many African nations, as well as the Muslim holy city of Mecca. During his visit to Mecca, Malcolm saw people of all races coming together in peace.

Malcolm's wife, Betty Shabazz, is shown here. She and his daughters were very important to him. It upset him when he found out that Elijah Muhammad didn't take being an honorable family man as seriously as he did.

He started to believe Black people and white people could work together.

Fast Fact

In 1964, Malcolm changed his name to El-Hajj Malik El-Shabazz.

A New Path

Malcolm came home from Mecca with new ideas about how to fight racism. He no longer believed all white people were evil. He saw Islam as the key to ending racism in the United States. He also expressed a new desire to work with other civil rights leaders.

Malcolm began to connect the fight for civil rights in the United States with the worldwide fight for human rights. He had a new mission, and it seemed he was ready to become a new kind of leader. However, the world never got to see if Malcolm's new outlook would have changed the civil rights movement.

Malcolm returned from Mecca more hopeful about the future.

THE ORGANIZATION OF AFRO-AMERICAN UNITY

In 1964, Malcolm helped create the Organization of Afro-American Unity (OAAU). Although Malcolm's previous organizations all had ties to Islam, this had no religious connection. Instead, the goal of the OAAU was to connect African Americans with Africans. The OAAU was based on the Organization of African Unity (OAU), which was a collection of African nations that provided a unified front on issues that affected the continent. Malcolm hoped the OAAU and OAU could work together.

The OAAU also focused on helping African Americans succeed in business and politics. It reflected Malcolm's growing understanding of the need for connection rather than separation.

Malcolm visited Africa and talked to leaders there about the problems in the United States.

Malcolm X's funeral was a sad day, but it wasn't the end of his story. His legacy lives on in many ways today.

GONE BUT NOT FORGOTTEN

Chapter Four

By 1965, Malcolm X seemed ready to start the next chapter in his story as a civil rights leader. However, the NOI actively tried to stop him from continuing his work. Malcolm faced death threats, and his house was set on fire. He knew he was in danger, but he kept speaking out.

A Life Cut Short

On February 21, 1965, Malcolm was supposed to give a speech in New York City. People filled the Audubon Ballroom to hear what he had to say. However, instead of witnessing a powerful speech, they witnessed a terrible tragedy. Three men shot and killed Malcolm while he was onstage. They were members of the NOI.

Malcolm's wife and their four daughters were there the night he was killed. A few months later, Betty gave birth to twin girls. They never got to meet their father.

Fast Fact

Workers often dig the grave in which a person is buried. However, Malcolm's friends did this sad job themselves.

THE SHABAZZ CENTER

The Audubon Ballroom was the site of Malcolm's death, but today, it's a place to learn more about his life. In 2005, the location that used to be the Audubon Ballroom was officially reopened as the Malcolm X & Dr. Betty Shabazz Memorial and Educational Center, which is often shortened to the Shabazz Center. Through a partnership with Columbia University, the Shabazz Center became a location for learning more about the life of Malcolm X and Dr. Betty Shabazz, who worked hard to honor her husband's legacy. Organizations and activist groups are also invited to use this space for events.

Shown here is a mural at the Shabazz Center that shows important moments in Malcolm's life.

Telling His Story

Malcolm's words continued to live on after his death. Not long after his assassination, *The Autobiography of Malcolm X* was published. An autobiography is a person's life story told in their own words. Malcolm had been working on his autobiography with writer Alex Haley for years before his death.

Fast Fact
Betty Shabazz died in 1997 after her grandson started a fire in her apartment.

The Autobiography of Malcolm X introduced the world to the details of Malcolm's life—from his childhood and time in prison to his views about race and racism. It helped Malcolm's ideas spread to even more people. Today, many people still read this book and study it in school.

Malcolm wrote his autobiography with help from Alex Haley, who's shown here. Haley later wrote the famous novel *Roots: The Saga of an American Family*, which traced a family Haley claimed was his from the time of slavery to the 1970s.

Fast Fact

In 1992, the movie *Malcolm X* became a huge hit and helped a new generation become more interested in Malcolm's story. The movie was directed by Spike Lee and starred Denzel Washington as Malcolm.

Shown here is Denzel Washington in *Malcolm X*, which is a movie that introduced even more people to Malcolm's story.

The Roots of Black Power

The ideas of Black pride, self-defense, and turning anger into action didn't die with Malcolm. In fact, they grew stronger after his death. Many of Malcolm's teachings became the foundations of the Black Power movement. This movement gained popularity in the late 1960s and 1970s and led to the creation of groups such as the Black Panther Party.

The Black Panther Party was a **militant** group. It carried on the ideas of self-defense and **self-reliance** that Malcolm had talked about. It did this by patrolling communities to defend against police violence and providing services such as health care and free breakfasts for children.

Malcolm's Message Today

Malcolm once said, "You can't separate peace from freedom because no one can be at peace unless he has his freedom." This message is still important today, as Black Americans continue to fight for their freedoms and rights.

Malcolm X's influence can be felt in the Black pride expressed by artists, writers, and others across the United States. It can be felt in the anger they express too. His words unlocked a new understanding of the Black American experience, and they're as meaningful today as they were more than 50 years ago.

Beyoncé is one of many artists who've been inspired by Malcolm X. She's included his words on her album *Lemonade* and in her concerts.

TIMELINE

In Malcolm's Life

1925
Malcolm Little is born on May 19 in Nebraska.

1946
Malcolm goes to prison.

1952
Malcolm leaves prison with a new last name—X.

1964
After cutting ties with the NOI, Malcolm starts the OAAU and Muslim Mosque, Inc.

1965
Malcolm is murdered on February 21, and later that year, *The Autobiography of Malcolm X* is published.

In the World

1929
The U.S. stock market crashes, beginning the Great Depression.

1939–1945
World War II is fought.

1950
The Korean War begins.

1963
Martin Luther King Jr. delivers his "I Have a Dream" speech.

1965
The Voting Rights Act of 1965 is passed to stop discrimination in voting based on race.

THINK ABOUT IT!

1. How do you think the events of Malcolm's childhood shaped his ideas about white people?

2. Why did some of Malcolm's speeches make people angry or uncomfortable? Why did they make others feel inspired?

3. Why did Malcolm disagree with some civil rights leaders?

4. Give an example of Malcolm's influence in the world today.

GLOSSARY

alternative: A choice or option.

boycott: The act of joining with others in refusing to deal with someone or support a business as a form of protest.

culture: The beliefs and ways of life of a certain group of people.

foster home: A household in which care is given to a child who has been taken from the home of their biological parents because they cannot care for their child.

integration: The practice of uniting people from different races; the opposite of segregation.

legacy: The lasting effect of a person or thing.

militant: Using force to support a cause or beliefs.

realistic: Likely to happen; based on what is real and not what is hoped for.

robbery: The act of stealing.

self-reliance: A feeling of trust someone has in their own abilities; the belief that someone can do something on their own.

FIND OUT MORE

Books

Hinton, Kerry. *The Black Power Movement and Civil Unrest*. New York, NY: Rosen Publishing, 2018.

Saidian, Siyavush. *Did the Civil Rights Movement Achieve Civil Rights?* New York, NY: PowerKids Press, 2019.

Stoltman, Joan. *Malcolm X*. New York, NY: Gareth Stevens Publishing, 2019.

Websites

ABC News: Malcolm X Through the Years
abcnews.go.com/US/photos/malcolm-years-29114886/image-29115811
Visitors to this website will find a collection of photos from throughout Malcolm X's life.

BrainPOP: Malcolm X
www.brainpop.com/socialstudies/famoushistoricalfigures/malcolmx/
This website features a video, a quiz, and other activities related to Malcolm X's life and work.

The Shabazz Center
theshabazzcenter.org/
You can plan a visit to the Shabazz Center using the information on its official website.

INDEX